BroKEn ChAIn
Bonus Poems
Included
By
S. E. McKenzie

i

DEDICATION
To everyone who has been left out in the cold.

TABLE OF CONTENTS

BROKEN CHAIN

I

In Ghetto Town
Everyone is standing around
Putting each other down.

The chain
Reaction;
Never ending

In satisfaction;

Alienation;
A hurt sensation;
Imprisoned by a generation

Without imagination;
Lost in a war;
Bad memories awake

When the broken hearted sleep;
So lost in the Negative Zone;
Losing their imagination

Was their first mistake.

They take what they can
As they bulldoze the rest;
Leaving many dispossessed.

In the Ghetto Town
Wearing a cross; wearing a frown;
Mean girls putting poor boys down.

"What isn't being replaced by a global,
Live and let die Economy?
Poor Boy asked to know one in particular;

Things were changing and were not so familiar;
Scaled; interconnected; global;
Sometimes silently;

Sometimes vocal;

Watchers stare;
They don't care;
They wave to the Mean Girls

Who are dressed for success.
They can't connect substantially
As they grow old locally;

BROKEN CHAIN: Bonus Poems Included

And so divided.

Downtown Streets
Growing into speedways;
Hostile to walkers and bikers.

Global impact;
A fact of life
That doesn't change;

Mean Girls
So vain and protected;
Never loved for themselves

Barbie Dolls
Sitting on shelves.
How they laugh

During the Mind War;
The war with no end
The mind; Infinite Space;

Without curiosity
Lost capacity
Generation without imagination;

Or anything;

Poor Boy has no place;
And how they laugh
While he is displaced;

Mean Girls carry their fear card;
In their tight blue jeans;
They catch poor boy off guard;

As they stress their targets out;
With accusations
Hear them shout;

"There is only one way out."

No defence; their eyes are everywhere;
They are watching;
Those ghettoized on the other side;

Social Disorder
Growth Industry
So the watchers can buy bling;

Off the street;
Across the sea;
Politics of Vanity;

How they watch but cannot see.
The growing gap
In a live and die economy.

How they watch and cannot see
The dispossessed and neglected;
Displaced and unprotected.

How they watch but cannot see;
As they exclude and collude
Destroying Poor Boy's will to live

"Only one way out"
They shout;
You will never fit

Into this closed knit
Society;
"Only one way out

Or die in anxiety."

The weapons of choice;
Worn Porn;
Destroys assumption of innocence;

Destroys common sense;
Social Order
Right side and wrong side

Of the Tracks
Behind the red line
Ghost suppliers

From who knows where
Secret Police dressed to kill
Dressed to thrill.

Sometimes like a mean girl
Who has never been loved for her self
Barbie Doll on a shelf

Poor boy willing to give love a try;
Born on the poor side of town;
Too young to give up and die;

The militarized police
Already know his face
Telling him to know his place;

City planning with class assumptions;
Social Disorder
As barriers on the dark side of town

Destroy civility somehow
Nowhere to cross
Accept under the bridge

Where the desperate are displaced;
The Mean Girls shout;
"There is only way out".

Mean Girls have never been loved
Just for themselves;
Barbie dolls sitting on shelves.

Poor Boy's

Ancestors were born in the Negative Zone too;
They too were excluded
While the cronies colluded.

Detained in concrete
As the Watchers wave
To the Mean Girls

Old money;
In bred style to
Impoverish those

If they don't go;
Pace is slow;
Small Town Culture

In a Big Box City;
Brutality
Is second nature

While toy guns
Are waved around
For fun

As the mean boys
From the pretty part of town
Run Poor Boys down;

BROKEN CHAIN: Bonus Poems Included

On the other side of the lights;
Rich Boys pick fights;
To fill the boring nights;

While they deaden their souls;
Loss of imagination
Lost in alienation

A hurt sensation

Standing on the other side of the street.
Poor Boys are under suspicion
Micromanaged to death

By cruel fools
Who don't follow their own rules;
The only growth industry

Is the fear of disorder
Everyone just feels sadder
Inside they feel madder;

While downtown streets
Grow into speedways;
The community hall

Is now a mall.
Mean Girls
Left church early

Looking so girly
With hair unnaturally curly;
They wave to the Watchers so burly.

Mean Girls strut
Then cross the street
To look for action and satisfaction;

II
The Watchers point out
Poor Boy without a cent.
Mean Girls get ready

To torment
And to manufacture consent.
Mean Girls are never loved for themselves;

BROKEN CHAIN: Bonus Poems Included

Just Barbie Dolls sitting on shelves.

The Watchers shout,
"We are the new global order,
Our authority knows no border.

We want all Poor Boys
Out of sight;
For this is Sunday night

And the mighty dollar
Has holy power
For those who pray for it everyday;

If you have none go away."
Poor Boy heard
The harsh words;

Brought on feelings of alienation
Medicalized
As a pathology without an apology;

Or common sense.

S.E. McKENZIE

For money had "in God we trust"
Written all over it
While it jingles

In the Watchers' pockets.
While the Mean Girls
Strut their stuff;

Had their noses up in the air;
Few could care
For the Mean Girls;
Even though their hearts raged;

Poor boys were being watched and processed
By the Militarized Police State;
With a pretty boy as its head;

Industry of alienation
A hurt sensation
For the indebted generation

Without imagination.

Indebted to old men
Getting ready to die
Going back to their home in the sky.

III

And on the fringe of Ghetto Town
Deer
Were still free; before they were shot.

They had no fear;
Even though
The Machine State was growing

While feeding from
Contracted funds
To Watch but never know

Those herded into skid row.

As affordable housing
Was bulldozed down
The militarized Watchers

Watched everyone in town;
Accept those in their clique;
There were allowed in the circle;

Allowed to speak.

The Watchers waved to the Mean Girls
Across the street
Who were kicking Poor Boy down;

He was from the poorest part of town;
The Mean Girls said
He filled us with fear

We would sue him if he had a penny to his name
But we will hurt him all the same
Poor Boy is the only one to blame;

So easy to forget his name.
He will wish he was never born;
Thanks to our weaponized porn.

BROKEN CHAIN: Bonus Poems Included

Money linked
Those who had it
To the chain;

And there was nothing much more
Left to link us together
Nothing much to gain but pain.

Barriers and round-abouts were placed

In the streets
To channel traffic
To the mall;

And on the fringe
Wild Life
Lived

But there was no plan
To curb market forces
Accept in our part of town.

S.E. McKENZIE

Barriers blocked access;
Legislated poverty;
Property in distress

In our upside down world.

Mean Girls and Watchers drove way too fast
Too dangerous to turn;
So they say;

Members from the coalition
Always get their way
Backing into traffic everyday;

Members of group think
Spin you around
In their loop;

Small town on a Sunday night;
Mean Girls kicking Poor Boys down
While growing old way too fast.

BROKEN CHAIN: Bonus Poems Included

Mean Girls never loved for themselves
Still doing it
In a car parked in the underpass.

Hate feeds
Alienation
From each other

Stress feeds
Alienation
From themselves.

As their teeth rot
Their belly grows
And they don't even notice;

Until it is too late
To change fate
While they call those

On the other side
Of the lights
Trash

Just because they have less cash
For they had been excluded
While the cronies colluded.

A long time ago; alienation;

Now the glass ceiling
Has become the floor
As we are all pushed through the revolving door

Once more.

Legislated poverty
Was never called by name
Neither was God.

IV

We all knew the impact just the same.
As the dead end street;
Were numbered; they had no name.

BROKEN CHAIN: Bonus Poems Included

Surrounded by parking lots
Encroached
On Nature's beauty.

Lost sense of civic duty.

Not planned for public good;
Devaluing property
Into a slum;

Treating us as if we were bums;
No longer Equity Tenants;
Assets

Are now toxic.
In the Negative Zone;
Thought you could never feel so alone.

No repair for this Urban Sprawl
One day it will be bulldozed
To make a playground

For the rich;
The wild life living on the fringe
Could only watch

While the Mean Girls
Feared those
They persecuted.

The unemployed
Were treated rough
And the hypocrisy caused feelings of rage.

The police state without connectors
Paved Paradise
The way we had been warned.

There was nowhere for children to play

Or for Nature to do her stuff;

V

Broken Chain
Man against Man
To control Means of Production;

Surplus from Production
Outcome of Production
Is no longer true

I saw how machines
Replaced you
Without a tear

Without a fear

While the Mean Girls
Standing at the front door
At the Local Dive

While their own worn porn
Destroyed love
For love was not that tough.

Accused you
Of being destitute
No tenderness at all.

Cultural Decline;
Very few
Knew their own minds.

Group think
Excluded those on the other side of the tracks
While the cronies colluded

In plain sight
On Sunday night
Everyone was uptight.

BROKEN CHAIN: Bonus Poems Included

As the Mean Girls
Picked a fight with Poor Boy,
Made Poor Boy feel hopeless;

Overnight;
And it was mostly the hypocrisy
That caused his heart to rage;

As he hung from the ceiling
He wondered why the world
Had lost all the good feeling

He felt as a boy;
Always a Poor Boys
But could still feel joy.

For he had the soul of a poet;
He saw beauty
Where others could not;

And he felt pain
When others would not;
And perhaps same soul

S.E. McKENZIE

Will fly
Into another Poor Boy
Too angry to die.

While the Mean Girls
Complained all day long
About those closest to them;

That were still living;
It was Sunday night
And the chain was broken;

Their pain had awoken;

Mean girls want to leave town
For a better life
But don't know how;

They were too afraid
Of progress
And only those that left

Soon came back
To the small town
Where their ancestors were born

Now feeling so worn;
They understood
How the town had regressed.

In all the spin
Many closed their eyes to survive
In the 'live and let die' global economy.

What had been lost;
Collective Consciousness
Excluded those on the other side of the lights.

Only the birds in the sky were free;

Mean Girls; rigid and blue;
Prejudice made them as cold as ice;
When they touched you.

It didn't feel nice.
Concluding and colluding
Fed their fear; the price;

Stayed with their own kind
They never knew their own mind;
Fought with those excluded.

Mean Girls; the Gate Keepers;
Laughed at the broken hearted.
The chosen few were certain to win.

For everyone knew

Manufacturing war-stuff
Was more profitable
Than filling the world with love.

THE END

Bonus Poems
Excerpted from
Haunted Poems
Hunted Shadows

GOLDEN WINGS

I was looking for my higher power,
I was looking for it all day,
The sun could not shine,
The clouds were in the way.

You were the one with the golden wings,
You flew into my life.
Like a shadow, you took away my breath,
As you led me out of this valley of death.

Then you covered me with your Golden wings,
You looked into my soul of fire,
You made me blind with desire,
And all I could do was close my eyes.

When I awoke in the middle of the night,
All I wanted to do was hold you tight,
But you left me all alone,
So I could grow wings of my own.

LOVE AND I

It was another day,
The sky was grey,
The clouds were in the way,
Of the sun's shine.

I know what is mine,
Love and I,
We try to believe,
So we give it another try.

Makes it all worthwhile,
To see you smile,
Love and I,
Hope it is not a lie.

ATOMIC ACHE

I don't want atomic Ache
Cause I wanna do it again
Again and again.

Love generates electricity,
In the maze of Relativity,
Please spare me your hate.

Hate is a communicable disease.
And Hate is so hard to please.
In the maze of Relativity.
Please spare me your hate.

I wanna hear your heart music so fine,
I wanna hear it real close to mine.
I know love generates electricity,
In the maze of relativity.

So don't get me con-fused.
Cause I don't want to be misused,
Cause I wanna do it again,
Again and again

MOTION

There is motion in Creation.
Like magic energy grows without explanation.
Was Motion meant to be lived?
As cycles can never be rushed,
You learn to be patient
And the creation will create itself.

There is motion in co-motion
That is felt quicker than words can explain?
Why is love so seldom thanked?
Is your love's strength being weakened by illusion?

So, let your soul flower bloom and feel that light,
Take the time, take all night.
As motion moves all around, floating in air,
Sometimes invisible, sometimes in full bloom,
I try to take it all in.

WHY I LOVE YOU

Oh, you came to me,
When I was all alone,
In a world as cold as stone,
That is why I love you.

You picked me up
When I was down,
You kissed away my frown,
That is why I love you.

You gave me a reason to dream,
While the world made me wanna scream,
You took my hand; I was under your command,
That is why I love you.

And if you should go away,
I will love you anyway,
You brought new meaning to my life
That is why I love you.

THE LITTLE GREEN THING

Hope for hope's sake,
To the tune of the Skin Drum,
Hoping for peace of mind,
While searching for the Little Green Thing

Lost during Rush Hour.
I wonder who knows
Where the Little Green Thing is.
It may have been blown away by all this rush,
Still I hope to draw upon its Holy Energy,

For the Little Green Thing has
Written "In God we Trust" All over it.
Within its hyper-active soul
The two faced God Head haunts you

While the Little Green Thing, Is still lost.
Now, you must really hope before you see,
The Little Green Thing alive,

It beats to the tune of the Skin Drum,
To the beat so slow but hard.
The little Green Thing is floating away
It is never able to stay.

THE D.R.A.F.T.

The D.R.A.F.T could tear you apart
Your stomach could fight your heart
Your brain could stop acting smart
As you become their human capital

D is for deadly
R is for response
A is for against
F is for free
T is for types

When I wrote that poem
I was thinking at home
Then just like before
You came knocking at my door

Now you say killing is wrong
Now you say you need a new song
Now you say you need me
But how can we love, when we aren't free?

A.W.O.L.

Can't fight this machine war,
Can't fight it any more.
I must stay here like this with you tonight,
To see your hair shine in the morning light.

I have seen what the machine can do
And it is breaking my heart in two.
I have seen the machine explode in their face,
I have seen their blood splattered all over the place.

I have crawled in the mud,
And I felt so cold,
I swam in the sea of blood,
I felt so old.

And I know
This is where
I must be
Sleeping beside you so peacefully.

I don't wanna fight this machine war
I don't wanna do it anymore.
I have seen some divide just to multiply,

A.W.O.L. (continued)

Others kill without hearing a cry.
Some justify this as they eat the pie,
And some mystify it all
cause they know the lie.

I must stay here
Beside you,
That's all
I really need to do.

Let me hide from this machine war,
Let me feel this peace I have never felt before.
I have missed Role-call.
I am now A.W.O.L.

With only one life to live
I must give all the love
I have to give.
I must stay here,

I must feel no fear.
While I am beside you,
Loving you.
This is what I was born to do.

NOUVEAU GESTAPO

It could have been love at first sight
Until you tried to flex your might.
You had eyes sometimes blue
And sometimes green,

As your gun made you look so mean.

He was born in a slum.
They called him a bum.
They said he was bad,
But I knew he was sad.

He had been in a cage,
I could feel his rage.
As it grew with age,
The future was forgotten,

Nouveau gestapo (continued)

While he just felt rotten,
He couldn't cope,
He needed dope,
The Gestapo's rope.

You were walking on your beat
He was walking on his street
He saw you, he started to run
You shot him, and then dropped your gun.

The street was red
Soaked with the blood
Gushing from his head
He was at peace,
Now he was dead.

THE END

Produced by S.E. McKenzie Productions
First Print Edition October 2015

Enquiries: 1(778)992-2453
Mailing Address:
S. E. McKenzie Productions
168 B 5th St.
Courtenay, BC
V9N 1J4

Email Address:
messidartha@aol.com

http://www.amazon.com/SarahMcKenzie/e/B00H9RWX48

www.ingramcontent.com/pod-product-compliance
Lightning Source LLC
Chambersburg PA
CBHW060543030426

42337CB00021B/4408